More Chat-up Lines and Put Downs

Stewart Ferris

SUMMERSDALE

Copyright © Stewart Ferris 1998

All rights reserved. No part of this book may be reproduced by any means, nor transmitted, nor translated into a machine language, without the written permission of the publisher.

Summersdale Publishers Ltd
46 West Street
Chichester
PO19 1RP
UK

ISBN 1 84024 046 6

Printed and bound in Great Britain.

Acknowledgements

Emma Burgess, RJ, Terry G, and LIBF Helen.

I can read you like a book. I bet you're great between the covers.

I'm not letting you anywhere near my spine.

More Chat-up Lines and Put Downs

What winks and is great in bed?

I don't know.

(Wink)

I'd like to father your children.

Fine, they're over there.

Would you like me to lick champagne out of your navel?

There isn't any in it.

More Chat-up Lines and Put Downs

You've turned my floppy disk
into a hard drive.

*Sorry, I don't date men
with tiny peripherals.*

What time would you like me to set
the alarm for in the morning?

*I don't care.
My boyfriend always gets me up.*

I'd like to make love to you.

I'd rather we skipped straight to the post-coital fag.

Would you like me to get into your knickers?

There's already one arsehole in there, and that's plenty.

More Chat-up Lines and Put Downs

Where have you been all my life?

What do you mean – I wasn't even born for the first half of it.

Would you like a f**k . . .

No.

. . . ing drink?

Do you want to come back to
my place for a pizza and a shag?

No thanks, I don't like pizza.

More Chat-up Lines and Put Downs

Do you sleep on your stomach?

No.

Can I, then?

Bond. James Bond.

Off. Piss off.

It's getting late. Why don't we have a shag?

No thanks, I'm too tired.

Well why don't you lie down while I have one?

The doctor said I should release
my fluids regularly. Would you mind
if I used your body as a receptacle?

I'll lend you a cup.

Your face or mine?

His.

Hey, don't go yet . . .
you've forgotten something.

What?

Me.

What sign were you born under?

'No entry'.

More Chat-up Lines and Put Downs

Excuse me, I'm new around here. Can you give me directions to your bedroom?

I'm not very good with directions. You'd better ask my boyfriend.

Wow.

Yuk.

Would you like to come back to my place for a bacardi and grope?

Just a gin and platonic, please.

Can you tell me the time, because I want to make a note of the moment we first met?

I'll give it to you twice, because it's also the moment we split up.

Excuse me, aren't we related?

No, and I don't want to be.

I know a great way to burn off the calories in that sandwich you've just eaten.

Yes, me too, and it involves running away from you.

You have the bluest eyes I've ever seen.

Thanks. I only had them resprayed yesterday.

You look like you've never done it in a water bed.

You look like you've never done it.

When I was a prisoner of war they tortured me on the rack, and it wasn't just my legs they stretched . . .

What else, then – your imagination?

Can I phone you for a date?
What's your number?

It's in the phone book.

But you haven't told me your name.

That's in the phone book, too.

Underneath these clothes
I'm completely naked.

Prove it . . . to someone else.

You're utterly beautiful, but there must be something about you that's less than perfect: I expect you're a hopeless cook.

True, so I suppose Nature's compensated you with perfect cooking abilities, then?

You remind me of the last person
I went out with.

That must be going back a bit.

Have you ever experienced puppy love?

*No, only pigeon-holing and
monkey-spanking.*

The best thing about you
would have to be my arms.

*Thanks – I would offer to shag your
brains out, but it looks as if
someone has beaten me to it.*

Excuse me, is your body real?

No. You have to inflate it through my mouth every ten minutes.

Can I count on your vote?

I doubt if you can even count.

(Call her over using your finger)
I made you come using just one finger. Imagine what I could do with my whole hand!

Can you make yourself come with just one finger?

I think the sun shines out of your arse.

Well, you're living proof that even a turd can be polished.

Excuse me, I want to be served by the most attractive waitress. You do work here, don't you?

No, I just serve pizzas for fun.

Do you know the difference between fellatio and focusing?

No.

Would you mind helping me adjust my telephoto lens, then?

This is an amazing coincidence . . .
I'm single on the day that we
meet for the first time.

*You'll still be single if we
ever meet again.*

Are you free tomorrow night?

No, but I'm on special offer the day after.

Congratulations! You've won first prize in a competition: a date with me!

Oh. What was second prize? Two dates with you?

Will you call me pretty soon?

I doubt it – you're not pretty now and I'd be surprised if that ever changed.

I'd go through anything for you.

Great, the exit's just over there.

If I could see you naked, I'd die happy.

If I could see you naked, I'd die.

Can I spend the evening with you?

I gave up baby-sitting years ago.

Can I buy you a drink?

I'd rather just have the cash.

What's a girl like you doing in a place like this?

Trying to avoid you.

Save me – I'm drowning
in a sea of love!

Tough, I can't swim.

God must have cried when
you left heaven.

*Yes, and he held a huge party
when you left.*

You and me would look sweet together on a wedding cake.

Only once you'd been cut in half.

You look good enough to eat.

What a shame you need to diet, then.

When I look at you, I know I've caught the love bug.

It's a pity you weren't inoculated.

Take that jacket off and
let me look at your spine.

*Come any closer and I'll
throw the book at you.*

I'd like to run my fingers
through your hair.

*Yes please – you can wipe
the lice on my sleeve.*

Seeing you makes my heart beat uncontrollably fast.

The sight of you gives me heart burn.

If you were a building you would be Versailles Palace.

And you'd be a shed.

Do you believe in magic?

I used to, until I realised I can't make you disappear.

Do you believe in love at first sight?

No.

We could make beautiful music together.

I'll just fetch my earplugs, actually.

I have designs on you.

*I think you'd better go back
to the drawing board.*

Can I bury my head in your cleavage?

Just bury your head.

You're the one I've been waiting for all my life.

Let's hope you die young.

You bring me out in a hot sweat.

You bring me out in an allergic rash.

I could get lost in your eyes.

*That's conjunctivitis,
it makes them a little foggy.*

Will you come out with me?

Out of the closet, certainly, because meeting you has helped me confirm my sexuality.

I want to be really dirty with you.

You smell as if you already are.

Am I the light of your life?

No, you're far too dim.

You make my heart skip a beat.

Only one? I was banking on a cardiac arrest.

More Chat-up Lines and Put Downs

I want to f**k you over and over again.

*I want to f**k you over.*

When should I phone you?

Whenever I'm not there.

I'm like quick-drying cement:
after I've been laid it doesn't take me
long to get hard.

*I'd rather go to bed with a
packet of cement.*

With me you need never fake an orgasm again.

With you I'd rather just fake the whole thing.

I don't expect to have sex with you on our first date. I'm quite restrained.

Well I'm even more restrained. I don't even expect to have a first date with you.

Sorry if I'm dribbling, but I had to get drunk before I could come and talk to you.

It's funny how pigs don't turn into men when they drink.

If you go out with me I'll treat you even better than my sports car.

What, a good servicing every ten thousand miles or every ten months, whichever comes first?

Where do you come from?

Way above your league.

Why don't we have a holiday romance?

*Most men like you remind me
of holidays . . . they never seem
to be long enough.*

More Chat-up Lines and Put Downs

Are you as hot as me?

I'm fine actually, but perhaps you should get some air to your brain by undoing your flies?

Shall we go to your place or mine?

Both. You go to yours and I'll go to mine.

Let's be honest with each other . . .
we've both come here for the
same reasons.

*Yes, you're right. Let's go and
pull some girls.*

You're most beautiful looking person I've ever seen.

So what makes you think I would want to talk to you, then?

When I'm with you I feel like a real man.

So do I.

Would you go crazy if I went out with you for a couple of months and then left you?

I'd go crazy if you went out with me for a couple of months and didn't *leave.*

More Chat-up Lines and Put Downs

If we went on a date, how would you describe me to your friends?

If I was desperate enough to date you, I wouldn't have any friends.

You'd probably regret it in the morning if we slept together, I suppose. So how about we sleep together in the afternoon?

Your approach wasn't bad, but I'd rather see your departure.

Excuse me, were you looking at me just then?

Yes, I thought from a distance you were good looking. Sorry, I forgot my glasses.

Can I be your love slave?

Well I certainly wouldn't pay you.

You've got such a heavenly body that I've named a star after you.

By the look of your body I wouldn't be surprised if someone had named a bouncy castle after you.

More Chat-up Lines and Put Downs

Look, I won't beat about your bush, I just want to get something fairly big between us.

How about the Atlantic Ocean?

I've always been fascinated by beautiful women. Mind if I study you?

Let's make it a joint project: I've always been fascinated by ugly men.

Hi, look, I'm not going to be able to date you tomorrow night, so why don't we squeeze one in tonight instead?

By the looks of you I doubt that it would be much of a squeeze.

I can fulfil your sexual fantasy.

Where's your horse, then?

Excuse me, would you help me with an itch that I can't reach?

Sure, just rub it against the lock on my chastity belt.

Can you help me? I had sex with someone last night, and I think it might have been you.

No, I think it was with yourself.

Hello, you don't know me, but I've just come back from the future in which you and me have the most passionate love affair. And it started tonight, actually.

And I've just come back from even further in the future where I found out that we're brother and sister, so let's change history, shall we?

You know, being a millionaire
can be pretty lonely without someone
to share it with.

*I'll share your money with you,
if you like.*

I'm sure I've noticed you before.

I'm not sure I've even noticed you yet.

Hi, I'm from Wonderbra. We're conducting free spot checks to make sure our customers are wearing the correct size bras. Just breathe out slowly once my hands are in place . . .

When you've done I'd better check your underpants. You look as if you could benefit from a smaller pair.

More Chat-up Lines and Put Downs

More Chat-up Lines and Put Downs

I feel like I already know you because I've undressed you completely in my mind. Nice body – I'd like to see more.

I did the same, but I wasn't impressed.

Would you like to go to bed with me tonight?

I can't – I haven't anything to wear.

I've got a condom
with your name on it.

*You must be mistaken. My name's not
Durex Extra Small.*

More Chat-up Lines and Put Downs

Would you like to wear real animal fur?

I would if it provided an extra layer between me and you.

Would you like to come to a concert with me?

I've got the CD.

I'm trying to break the world kissing record for snogging the most beautiful women in one evening. Can I kiss you?

Yes, but only because I'm trying to snog as many ugly men as possible tonight, and you would be worth double points.

You've got great boobs.

So have you.

You really set me on fire.

Oh good, I didn't think I used enough petrol.

If love is a drug, I'm addicted to you.

I recommend cold turkey.

What's your birthstone?

Breezeblock.

More Chat-up Lines and Put Downs

My body's like a temple.

I'd have said it was more like an amusement park.

I could really turn you on.

It's no big deal. I can do it myself just by not thinking about you.

Would you like to come for a meal with me next week?

I've eaten.

Mind if I take your picture?

Where to?

Can I take you on a shopping trip?

Wouldn't you rather just take me in bed?

Would you like to come to bed with me?
I've got an electric blanket.

*Why don't you come home with me
instead? I've got an electric chair.*

I would like to taste the salt
of the ocean on your lips.

Why don't you just eat a winkle?

Would you like to come to a nudist camp with me – I could show you what I've got to offer?

I could see that sort of thing in a packet of shrimps.

Can I wash your car for you?

I don't think your hose would reach.

Would you like to watch a sunset with me?

I've already seen one.

Can I fill you up, madam?

Unleaded, please.

Can I tickle your tonsils?

I think the surgeon has chucked them out.

Let me have a quick stroke.

Sure, shall I call the ambulance?

I'd like to have your children.

Go ahead and take them.

People think I'm a policeman because of the size of my love truncheon.

Yes, I remember 'Inch High Private Eye'.

My yacht is stranded here for a few days until the weather improves. Want to keep me company on it?

That depends on the size of your tender.

Will you hold my beer while
I go to the toilet?

Not while it's coming out, thank you.

I don't think I've seen you
for about ten years.

*Well make the most of it, because
with a bit of luck I won't see you
for another ten.*

Will you help me choose some garden furniture at the weekend?

I've already chosen some.

I'd like to jump into a bed with you.

OK, what about that flower bed?

Do you want to go clubbing with me?
Great, where can we find some seals?

You take my breath away.
I try, but you keep on breathing again.

Can I look up your skirt?

Certainly. Here's the catalogue. It's on page 57.

Would you like to come for a drink with me next week?

I'm not thirsty.

Can I pinch your bum?

Can I pinch your wallet?

You're irresistible.

You're resistible.

Didn't we meet in a past life?

Yes, and I wouldn't shag you then, either.

Would you like to come to a hilltop with me next week to watch the return of a comet that hasn't been visible for the last thousand years?

I've seen it.

Are you a policeman, or am I wrong in thinking that's a truncheon?

Both . . . I am a policeman, and it's not a truncheon.

How would you like my eggs in the morning?

Fertilised, please.

What's it like being the most attractive person here?

You'll never know.

The more I drink, the prettier you get.

There isn't enough alcohol on the planet to make me find you attractive.

I think we should leave together for the sake of the other women . . . you're making them look ugly.

Good idea. You're making the men look too good.

There's something on your face, I think it's beauty. Let me try and get it off . . . oh, it's not coming off.

Beauty shares the same characteristics as my bra. It's not coming off.

You make me melt like ice cream, you make me boil like a kettle, and you make me gurgle like the morning after a curry.

You need medical attention.

Let me put some fizz into your life.

OK, start by fixing my Sodastream.

I may be a bit of an eyesore, but beauty is only a light switch away.

You owe me a drink: you're so ugly I dropped my glass when I saw you.

Wasn't that you on the cover of Cosmo?

Yes, but I've finished sitting on it now. Want to borrow it?

I like to think it's my vocation to make women happy in bed.

Let me guess: you deliver meals on wheels to the bed-bound?

I'd like to demonstrate to you the
sexual equivalent of a marathon.

Go ahead. I'll just watch from over there.

You make me drunk with passion, intoxicated with love, and inebriated with desire.

Are you absolutely sure it's got nothing to do with the ten pints you've drunk tonight?

Can I see your tits?

No, they've just migrated.

Do you want to play my organ?

Only if it's got some good rhythms.

I'd like to watch you take your clothes off.

Off what?

Would you like to come for a meal with me?

No thanks, I'm anorexic.

Fancy a champagne breakfast?

Yes please. Get it delivered to me tomorrow.

Fancy a takeaway?

I wish someone would take you away.

Has anyone ever told you
how beautiful you are?

Yes, loads of people.

I've had part of my body pierced.
Would you like to know which bit?

Your brain.

Why not be original and say yes?

No.

More Chat-up Lines and Put Downs

I could make you the happiest woman on earth.

Why, are you about to go into space?

I'd like to marry you.

I'd rather skip straight towards the divorce.

I'm a postman, so you can rely
on me to deliver a large package.

*Sorry, but I need someone who comes
more than once a day.*

I bet you a drink that you won't kiss me.

You win. Here's a drink.

You're cute.

My cute what?

I bet you my watch that you won't let me grope you.

You win. Here's my watch.

Do you believe in love at first sight, or should I walk past you again?

Get yourself some sturdy walking boots.

I bet you my car that you won't have sex with me.

You win. Here's my car key.

Shall I open the door for you?

I'd rather you waited until we land.

I bet you my chest that you
won't take your bra off.

Sorry, I'm not playing anymore.

Would you like my seat?

*I didn't realise transplant surgery
was so advanced.*

Hey, it's you! I nearly didn't recognise you with your clothes on. Oh, sorry, I thought you were an ex-lover.

And I thought you were a future lover . . . until you opened your mouth.

Hello, I'm your cake. Would you like to have it or eat it?

I'm not hungry. I think I'll just give it to the dog.

I'd like to share with you my passion for squash.

I'm not thirsty.

You've lit my fuse, I'm going to explode with passion.

Perhaps if we put your little fuse somewhere wet it might go out?

I'm thinking of giving celibacy a try.

Not with me, you're not.

What radio station would you like me to switch on in the morning?

Hospital radio.

I'd like to lick your belly-button . . . from the inside.

Sure. Just don't burst any boils while you're there.

You look like a horse, and I'm a hedge. Would you like to jump me?

I think pruning would be a better idea.

Mind if I plug my lap-top into your modem socket?

Isn't amazing how small they can make them, these days?

More Chat-up Lines and Put Downs

I'm a helicopter pilot: fancy riding my chopper?

I'd rather just shag you.

Ever wanted to de-flower a virgin?

Nope.

112

It's not how big it is, it's what you can do with it that counts.

Well, you can certainly do something amazing: you can make it almost invisible to the naked eye.

More Chat-up Lines and Put Downs

If you kiss me I promise not to turn into a frog.

Why would I want to kiss you, then?

When I was a prisoner of war, held captive in a tower, the other men used part of me to climb down the wall and escape.

Oh no, not you again?

I think it's time we introduced ourselves.

I already know myself.

I'm learning to be an artist and
I'd like to paint you.

Sure, what colour?

I was planning on having sex tonight. Would you like to join me?

I can't make it tonight. You'll have to make it a rehearsal.

If I kissed you I'd go weak at the knees.

That's probably because I'd have just given you a good kicking.

You're very attractive even though if you were any more vacuous your head would implode.

If you were a little bit more intelligent you'd still be stupid.

If I told you I was well endowed
in the undercarriage department,
would you shag me?

No.

Good, because I'm
actually very small.

Are you from Jamaica?
Because Jamaican me crazy about you.

No, I'm from St Lucia.

Am I lost? I thought paradise
was further south.

*Yes, you should have turned left at the
roundabout, then take the second right.
You can't miss it.*

If you were food, you'd be caviar. If you were a word you'd be serendipity. If you were a car you'd be a Rolls Royce.

If you were a real man I might stay and talk to you.

Are you cold, or are you smuggling tic-tacs inside your bra?

Are you cold or are you smuggling a tic-tac inside your underpants?

Women say I have the gift of the gab.

Wrap it up, then.

You remind me of a squirrel. I'd like to pile my nuts up against you.

You remind me of a rat, and I've already called the Pest Control department.

Would you like to see something swell?

Yes, the bruise I'm about to inflict on your face.

Would you mind if I take your temperature using my special thermometer?

I always bite thermometers.

I love you.

I love chocolate, but I wouldn't bother chatting it up.

What would you say to a little f**k?

*Leave me alone, little f**k.*

Nice legs. When do they open?

Nice mouth. When does it shut?

Other Humour Books from Summersdale

Chat-up Lines and Put Downs
Stewart Ferris — £3.99

How To Chat-up Women (Pocket edition)
Stewart Ferris — £3.99

How To Chat-up Men (Pocket edition)
Kitty Malone — £3.99

Enormous Boobs
The Greatest Mistakes In The History of the World
Stewart Ferris — £4.99

101 Uses for a Losing Lottery Ticket
Shovel/Nadler — £3.99

Men! Can't Live with them, Can't live *with* them
Tania Golightly — £3.99

Girl Power
Kitty Malone — £3.99

The Kama Sutra For One
O'Nan and P. Palm — £3.99

101 Reasons Not To Do Anything
A Collection of Cynical and Defeatist Quotations — £3.99

A Little Bathroom Book £3.99

Available from all good bookshops.